All Around
Florida
Regions and Resources

Bob Knotts

Heinemann Library
Chicago, Illinois

© 2003 Heinemann Library
a division of Reed Elsevier Inc.
Chicago, Illinois

Customer Service 888-454-2279

Visit our website at www.heinemannlibrary.com

Designed by Heinemann Library
Page layout by Wilkinson Design
Printed and bound in the United States by
Lake Book Manufacturing, Inc.

07 06 05 04 03
10 9 8 7 6 5 4 3 2 1

**Library of Congress
Cataloging-in-Publication Data**

Knotts, Bob.
   All around Florida : regions and resources / Bob
Knotts.
      v. cm. -- (State studies)
Contents: The beautiful Sunshine State -- The Pan-
handle -- Northeast
Florida -- Central Florida -- Southwest Florida --
Southeast Florida --
The Keys.
   ISBN 1-40340-346-5 (HC) -- ISBN 1-40340-562-X
(PB)
   1. Florida--Geography--Juvenile literature. 2.
Florida--Description
and travel--Juvenile literature. 3. Regionalism--
Florida--Juvenile
literature. [1. Florida.] I. Title. II. State studies
(Heinemann
Library (Firm))
   F311.8 .K58 2002
   917.59--dc21
                                                    2002005697

Acknowledgments
The author and publishers are grateful to the
following for permission to reproduce copyright
material:

Cover photographs by (top, L-R) Scenics of
America/PhotoLink/PhotoDisc, Stephen J. Nesius/
Heinemann Library, Stephen J. Nesius/Heinemann
Library, Stephen J. Nesius/Heinemann Library,
(main) Franz-Marc Frei/Corbis; title page (L-R)
Stephen Frink/Corbis, Kevin Fleming/Corbis,
Stephen J. Nesius/Heinemann Library; contents
page (L-R) Peter Cosgrove/AP/Wide World Photo,
Hans Deryk/AP/Wide World Photo; pp. 4, 7T, 13,
19B, 21, 26, 27B, 28, 30B, 33, 39B Stephen J.
Nesius/Heinemann Library; pp. 5, 6, 8, 9, 11, 15T,
16T, 20T, 21B, 25, 26T, 31T, 32T, 35B, 37T, 43T,
45 maps.com/Heinemann Library; p. 7BL F. Stuart
Westmorland/Photo Researchers; pp. 7BR, 14, 17T,
22, 24, 37, 38, 39T Tony Arruza; p. 10 Jeff
Foott/Bruce Coleman, Inc.; pp. 12, 44B Jeff
Greenberg/Photo Edit; pp. 15, 18, 20 M. Timothy
O'Keefe/Bruce Coleman, Inc.; p. 16 Melissa
Farlow/National Geographic Image Collection;
pp. 17B, 23 Nik Wheeler/Corbis; p. 19T Andrew
Rakoczy/Bruce Coleman, Inc.; p. 27T Peter
Cosgrove/AP/Wide World Photos/Disney
Characters©Disney Enterprises, Inc. Used by
permission from Disney Enterprises, Inc.; pp. 29,
30T Farrell Grehan/Corbis; p. 31 Visit Florida;
p. 32 Dr. M.P. Kahl/Bruce Coleman, Inc.; p. 34
Alan Diaz/AP/Wide World Photo; p. 35 Phil
Sandlin/AP/Wide World Photo; p. 36 Stephen
Frink/Corbis; p. 40T Marta Garcia; p. 40B Greater
Fort Lauderdale Convention and Visitors Bureau;
p. 41T Larry Mulvehill/Corbis; p. 41B Dave G.
Houser/Corbis; p. 42 Bob Krist/Corbis; p. 43 Dave
Martin/AP/Wide World Photo; p. 44T Len Kaufman

Photo research by Julie Laffin

Special thanks to Charles Tingley of the
St. Augustine Historical Society for his comments
in the preparation of this book.

Every effort has been made to contact copyright
holders of any material reproduced in this book.
Any omissions will be rectified in subsequent
printings if notice is given to the publisher.

Some words are shown in bold, **like this.**
You can find out what they mean by looking
in the glossary.

Contents

The Sunshine State

Welcome to Florida! In Florida, you can learn about the history of this country's earliest European settlers in St. Augustine. You can spend time at Walt Disney World in Orlando, one of the most popular attractions in the entire world. You can learn about Florida's plants, animals, and environment in the more than 100 state and national parks. You can find out why Florida's climate makes it the nation's largest citrus grower. You can even discover how scientists are building the **International Space Station** with a trip to Kennedy Space Center in Cape Canaveral. In our travels around Florida's six **distinct** regions, you'll learn all this and much, much more.

Florida's warm climate helps two of its largest industries—the citrus and tourist industries.

FLORIDA'S LOCATION

Florida is located in the farthest southeastern corner of the **continental United States.** Water touches Florida

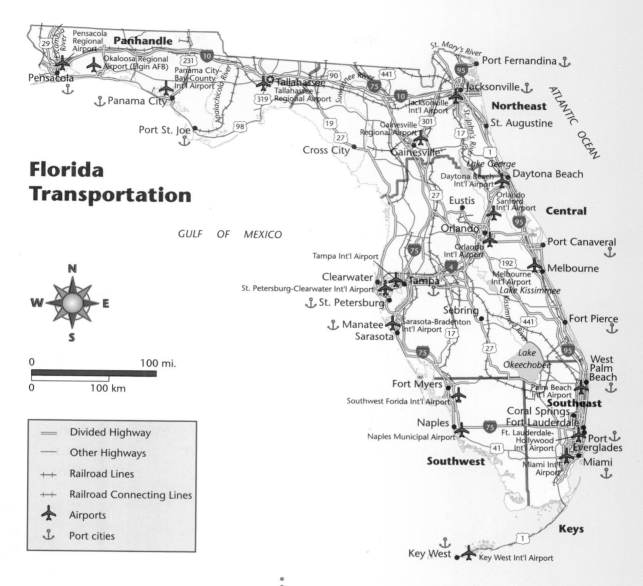

Florida Transportation

GULF OF MEXICO

N
W E
S

0 ———————— 100 mi.
0 ———————— 100 km

═══	Divided Highway
───	Other Highways
+++	Railroad Lines
+++	Railroad Connecting Lines
✈	Airports
⚓	Port cities

Panhandle

Pensacola Regional Airport
Okaloosa Regional Airport (Elgin AFB)
Pensacola
Panama City-Bay-County Int'l Airport
Panama City
Port St. Joe

Tallahassee
Tallahassee Regional Airport
Cross City
Gainesville Regional Airport
Gainesville
Eustis

Port Fernandina
Jacksonville
Jacksonville Int'l Airport
Northeast
St. Augustine
ATLANTIC OCEAN

Lake George
Daytona Beach Int'l Airport
Daytona Beach
Orlando Sanford Int'l Airport
Central
Orlando
Orlando Int'l Airport
Port Canaveral
Melbourne Int'l Airport
Melbourne
Lake Kissimmee
Fort Pierce

Tampa Int'l Airport
Clearwater
St. Petersburg-Clearwater Int'l Airport
Tampa
St. Petersburg
Manatee
Sarasota-Bradenton Int'l Airport
Sarasota
Sebring

Lake Okeechobee
West Palm Beach
Palm Beach Int'l Airport
Southeast
Coral Springs
Fort Lauderdale
Ft. Lauderdale-Hollywood Int'l Airport
Port Everglades
Miami Int'l Airport
Miami

Fort Myers
Southwest Forida Int'l Airport
Naples
Naples Municipal Airport
Southwest

Keys
Key West
Key West Int'l Airport

on three sides, which makes the land a peninsula. Florida's coast is about 1,200 miles long, longer than any other state except Alaska. The Atlantic Ocean washes against the state's east coast. The Gulf of Mexico, which is really a part of the Atlantic Ocean, laps against the western and southern coasts. The only land that touches Florida is to the north and northwest: Georgia and Alabama.

Florida has major roadways, along with port cities, railroads, and airports. Interstate Highway 75, which runs the length of Florida, actually starts in northern Michigan.

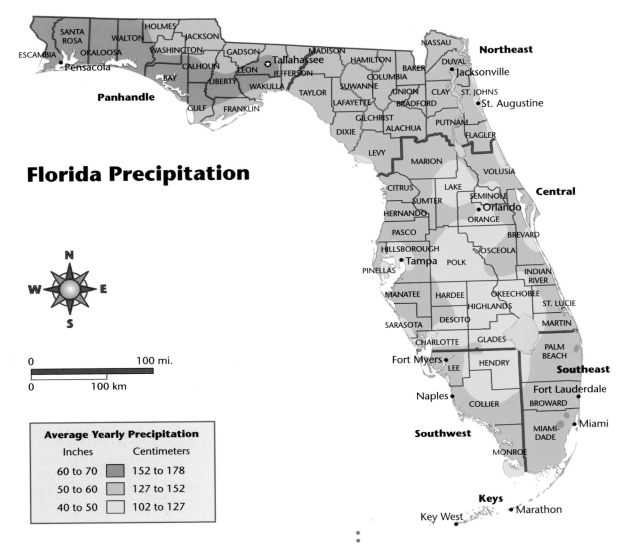

Florida Precipitation

Average Yearly Precipitation

Inches		Centimeters
60 to 70		152 to 178
50 to 60		127 to 152
40 to 50		102 to 127

Florida typically receives more annual precipitation than all other states except for Alabama, Hawaii, Minnesota, Montana, and parts of California.

Miami, in southeastern Florida, is closer to Havana, Cuba, than it is to Florida's capital of Tallahassee in the Panhandle.

Florida lies so far south that it is only about 100 miles above the **tropical** zone. The area of the world that includes Florida is called **subtropical.** Because of its location, Florida's weather is usually warm and sunny. This sunny climate has earned it the nickname of the

The ocean is an important part of Florida. It attracts tourists from around the world and provides food for many of Florida's people.

"Sunshine State." This climate has also attracted many residents and visitors.

Many people live in large cities along the coast, including Miami, Fort Lauderdale, Jacksonville, and Tampa. Orlando, in the center of Florida, is another large city. Plenty of people live in smaller towns, too, such as Micanopy, Apalachicola, or Mount Dora.

Orlando (below) and Jacksonville (right) are two of Florida's largest cities.

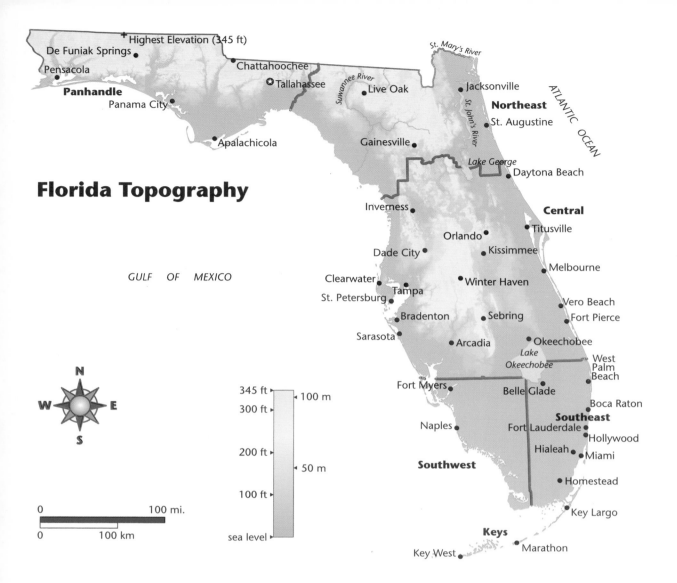

Florida Topography

Highest Elevation (345 ft)
De Funiak Springs
Pensacola
Panhandle
Panama City
Chattahoochee
Tallahassee
Live Oak
Suwannee River
St. Mary's River
Jacksonville
Northeast
St. Augustine
ATLANTIC OCEAN
Apalachicola
Gainesville
St. John's River
Lake George
Daytona Beach
Inverness
Central
Titusville
Orlando
Kissimmee
Dade City
Melbourne
Clearwater
Tampa
Winter Haven
GULF OF MEXICO
St. Petersburg
Bradenton
Sebring
Vero Beach
Fort Pierce
Sarasota
Arcadia
Okeechobee
Lake Okeechobee
West Palm Beach
Fort Myers
Belle Glade
Boca Raton
Naples
Fort Lauderdale
Southeast
Hollywood
Hialeah
Miami
Southwest
Homestead
Key Largo
Keys
Key West
Marathon

N W E S

345 ft
300 ft
200 ft
100 ft
sea level
100 m
50 m

0   100 mi.
0   100 km

Florida's lowest elevation—sea level—can be found around its entire coastline.

WHAT DOES FLORIDA LOOK LIKE?

While parts of Florida's land roll in gentle hills, the state is generally flat. Its highest point, Britton Hill in the town of Lakewood, is only 345 feet above sea level. Florida's highest point is the lowest of all of the states in this country.

The state of Florida is larger than some countries, such as England or Cuba. People need about eleven hours to drive from the top of the peninsula to the bottom. They need another three hours to reach Key West, the

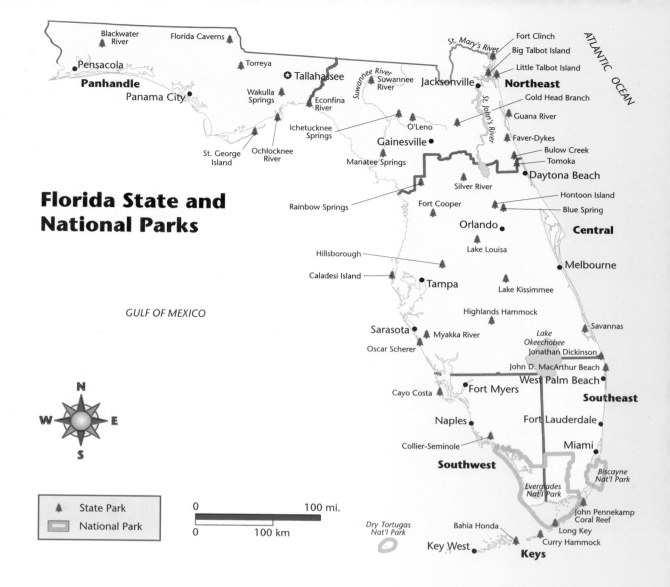

Florida State and National Parks

Map labels:

Blackwater River · Florida Caverns · Pensacola · **Panhandle** · Torreya · ⚑ Tallahassee · Panama City · Wakulla Springs · Econfina River · Suwannee River · Suwannee River · St. Mary's River · Fort Clinch · Big Talbot Island · Little Talbot Island · Jacksonville · **Northeast** · ATLANTIC OCEAN · Gold Head Branch · Guana River · St. John's River · O'Leno · Ichetucknee Springs · St. George Island · Ochlocknee River · Manatee Springs · Gainesville · Faver-Dykes · Bulow Creek · Tomoka · Daytona Beach · Rainbow Springs · Silver River · Fort Cooper · Hontoon Island · Blue Spring · Orlando · **Central** · Lake Louisa · Melbourne · Hillsborough · Caladesi Island · Tampa · Lake Kissimmee · **GULF OF MEXICO** · Highlands Hammock · Savannas · Sarasota · Myakka River · Oscar Scherer · Lake Okeechobee · Jonathan Dickinson · John D. MacArthur Beach · West Palm Beach · Cayo Costa · Fort Myers · **Southeast** · Naples · Fort Lauderdale · Collier-Seminole · Miami · **Southwest** · Biscayne Nat'l Park · Everglades Nat'l Park · John Pennekamp Coral Reef · Dry Tortugas Nat'l Park · Bahia Honda · Long Key · Curry Hammock · Key West · **Keys**

Compass: N W E S

Legend:
🔺 State Park
▭ National Park

0 ——— 100 mi.
0 ——— 100 km

westernmost island in the Florida Keys. Florida's long coastline has many beaches, which stretch out for a total of 663 miles. Florida's interior is marked by much undeveloped land, including over 100 state and national parks.

From Pensacola to Key West, the Florida State Park system offers 157 parks to the public.

Florida is a very wet state. It has more than 25 percent of the country's major **springs.** There are nearly 8,000 lakes larger than 10 acres in Florida. The biggest of these is Lake Okeechobee in central Florida. This lake is 35 miles long—more than 500 football fields! It is so long that you cannot see one end from the other.

Many people believe that the St. John's River is one of the best places in the country to catch bass.

There are also many rivers and canals throughout the state. Florida's largest river is the St. John's River. It flows north through the northeastern and central parts of the state. The river is 273 miles long. The Everglades are located in the southern regions of Florida. This large, wet area is home to alligators, crocodiles, and other **unique** animals.

FLORIDA'S ECONOMY

Florida's **subtropical** location is responsible for its climate. The climate attracts millions of tourists every year from all over the world. Therefore, Florida's important tourist economy depends a lot on the state's

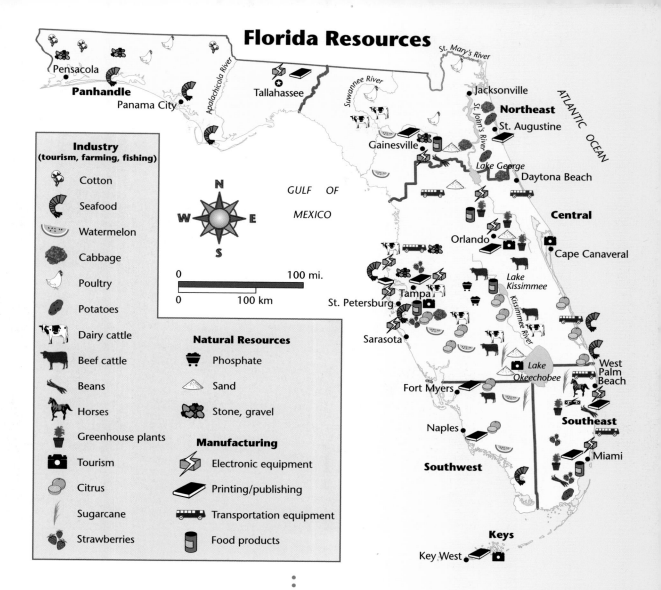

Florida Resources

Industry
(tourism, farming, fishing)

- Cotton
- Seafood
- Watermelon
- Cabbage
- Poultry
- Potatoes
- Dairy cattle
- Beef cattle
- Beans
- Horses
- Greenhouse plants
- Tourism
- Citrus
- Sugarcane
- Strawberries

Natural Resources

- Phosphate
- Sand
- Stone, gravel

Manufacturing

- Electronic equipment
- Printing/publishing
- Transportation equipment
- Food products

GULF OF MEXICO

ATLANTIC OCEAN

Panhandle — Pensacola, Panama City, Tallahassee

Northeast — Jacksonville, St. Augustine, Gainesville, Lake George, Daytona Beach

Central — Orlando, Cape Canaveral, Lake Kissimmee

Southwest — Tampa, St. Petersburg, Sarasota, Fort Myers, Naples, Lake Okeechobee

Southeast — West Palm Beach, Miami

Keys — Key West

location. Stores, restaurants, and other businesses in Florida pay many local workers to help the tourists. These workers then spend their money in other Florida stores and businesses. This makes Florida's economy strong. That is the reason why beaches and sunshine are among Florida's most important **natural resources.**

One of every three workers in Florida has a job in the service **industry,** such as waiting tables, driving taxis, or working in stores. These jobs depend on serving the public. Florida's tourist industry is the main reason for this. Sixty million tourists visit Florida each year. They

*Florida's resources are very **diverse.** Some are natural, such as **phosphate.** Others, like electronic equipment, are man-made.*

*Hundreds of thousands of Floridians work in the service **industry**.*

eat in restaurants, shop in stores, and ride tour boats. Residents also need these services. Restaurants and other businesses make most of their money from people who live in Florida. This helps create even more service jobs.

But Florida is much more than a place of tourists and beaches. It is a busy state where residents work in many types of jobs. Some Floridians, or people who live in Florida, grow oranges or other citrus fruit. Florida produces more citrus than any other state. Other Floridians grow vegetables or sugarcane.

Florida's gross state product is one of the highest in the country.

There are people who raise cattle on wide-open ranches, or cut down trees for **timber.** Some workers mine for **minerals** such as **phosphate.** Others take boats into the ocean to fish for

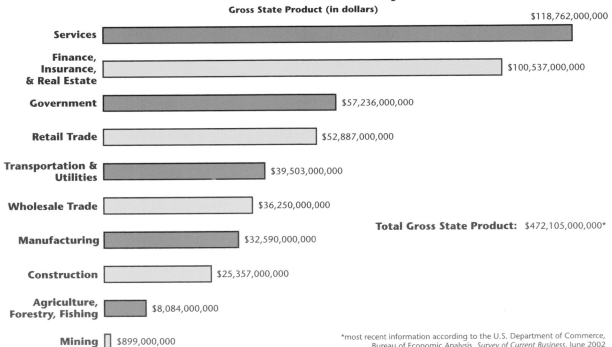

The Florida Economy
Gross State Product (in dollars)

Services	$118,762,000,000
Finance, Insurance, & Real Estate	$100,537,000,000
Government	$57,236,000,000
Retail Trade	$52,887,000,000
Transportation & Utilities	$39,503,000,000
Wholesale Trade	$36,250,000,000
Manufacturing	$32,590,000,000
Construction	$25,357,000,000
Agriculture, Forestry, Fishing	$8,084,000,000
Mining	$899,000,000

Total Gross State Product: $472,105,000,000*

*most recent information according to the U.S. Department of Commerce, Bureau of Economic Analysis, *Survey of Current Business*, June 2002

Tarpon Springs, on the Gulf of Mexico, is one of many Florida communities that depends on the ocean.

snapper, or catch shrimp and oysters. Floridians also make electronic products, chemicals, and paper in large factories.

FLORIDA'S SIX REGIONS

Each of Florida's six main regions, while different, has much to offer. The land, water, and resources are **distinct** in each of the regions, as are the industries, cities, and towns. Come along as we travel around the beautiful and exciting Sunshine State. We'll begin in the panhandle. Then, we'll move from northeast to central Florida. Next we'll go to southwest and southeast Florida. Finally, we'll end in the Keys. The state of Florida is waiting for you!

Florida, Then and Now

When the French explorer Jean Ribault arrived in Florida in 1562, he wrote that it was "the fairest, fruitfullest, and pleasantest of all the world, abounding in honey, venison, wildfowl, forests, [and] woods of all sorts." Some people would say that this still describes the Florida of today.

The Panhandle

The Florida panhandle is the area in the northwest part of the state. It gets its name from its shape, which looks like the handle of a frying pan.

The states of Alabama and Georgia sit on the panhandle's borders to the north and west. Part of the panhandle is in the Central Standard Time Zone, which is one hour earlier than the rest of Florida in the Eastern Time Zone. Cars are the main source of transportation, but there are also airports in Tallahassee and Pensacola. Many roadways, such as the I-10, run through the panhandle.

The panhandle is covered in pine and oak forests that are rooted in red clay soil. Florida has more than 15 million acres of forest.

THE LAND AND WATER

Much of the panhandle is made up of rolling hills. Some parts, like the half-million-acre Apalachicola National Forest, are so **dense** with trees that it would be easy to get lost there.

The panhandle has many **springs.** One of these is Wakulla Springs, which is one of the largest and deepest natural springs on Earth. There are also swamps, lakes, and rivers, including Little Porter Lake, the Apalachicola River, and the Yellow River. A **hydroelectric dam** is in the city of Chattahoochee.

The best-known part of the panhandle is its shoreline along the Gulf of Mexico. Some of the state's most famous beaches, including Panama City Beach, are here. Over millions of years, the sand was carried there by water from the **Appalachian Mountains.** It is nearly pure **quartz.** When you walk on it, you'll hear it squeak!

RESOURCES AND AGRICULTURE

The panhandle often has Florida's hottest and coldest weather. Monticello holds the state's record high of 109°F, and Tallahassee holds the state's record low of –2°F. The typical high in August is nearly 93°F. The low in January averages around 44°F. This region gets much less rainfall than many parts of Florida. Agriculture is not a main contributor to the economy here, although some cotton is grown.

Florida Panhandle Topography

Highest Elevation (345 ft)

Pensacola

Apalachicola River

Tallahassee

Panama City

Apalachicola

345 ft
300 ft
← 100 m
200 ft
← 50 m
100 ft
sea level

N
W   E
S

0   100 mi.
0   100 km

Florida's highest point, 345 feet above sea level, is in the panhandle. It is near the town of Lakewood, just south of the Alabama state line.

Millions of people visit the panhandle's beaches every year. This beach, at Seaside, Florida, is an important resource for the region.

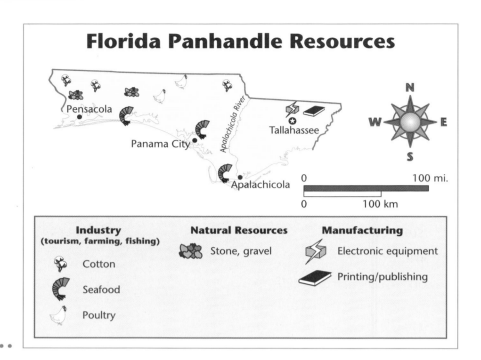

Florida Panhandle Resources

Pensacola

Panama City

Apalachicola River

Tallahassee

Apalachicola

N W E S

0   100 mi.
0   100 km

Industry
(tourism, farming, fishing)

Cotton

Seafood

Poultry

Natural Resources

Stone, gravel

Manufacturing

Electronic equipment

Printing/publishing

There is little agriculture in the panhandle, though some farmers grow cotton, tobacco, and peanuts, or raise hogs. Soybeans and corn also contribute to the region's economy.

INDUSTRY

Citizens of the panhandle depend on tourism (more than seven million people visit each year), lumber, and **commercial** fishing to make money. Boats search the seas for fish such as snapper and grouper. **Charter boats** take sport fishermen out in search of game fish, which are large fish that are difficult to catch. The town of Destin is home to Florida's largest charter boat fleet.

*Hardwood and **pulp** are turned into products like paper, plywood, and furniture. This **industry** provides jobs for more than 30,000 workers, including lumberjacks and truck drivers.*

Oystering in Apalachicola

The panhandle town of Apalachicola is known for the amount of oysters harvested there. Nine out of ten oysters eaten in Florida come from the waters around this community.

The state and federal government **employ** thousands of people in this region. Many of them live near the state capital of Tallahassee, where they carry out the challenging job of making Florida's laws work. Others who work for the government live on military bases, such as the Pensacola Naval Air Station or Eglin Air Force Base.

Finally, many of the panhandle's workers are in the health-care **industry.** In this region, more than 8,000 people work in hospitals and offices to support this industry.

Pensacola has several historic districts that people can visit to learn more about the long history of the city.

Tallahassee University Life

Around 25,000 college students live in Tallahassee each year.

Florida State University, or FSU, is a school well-known for research. FSU is also known as the most **wired** university in Florida. Florida Agricultural and Mechanical University, or FAMU, was established in 1887 as the state's major college for African Americans. Today, its resources include the Black Archives Research Center and Museum and a center for music and fine arts.

CITIES AND TOWNS

Panama City attracts thousands of college students each year for vacations. People can take dolphin tours here, where they pay to swim with these intelligent, gray sea mammals.

In Tallahassee, the new, 22-story capitol building sits directly next to the old capitol building, which is more than 150 years old.

Tallahassee also offers the Museum of Florida History and the Tallahassee Museum of History and Natural Science. This city museum includes a 52-acre wilderness area.

Many of the panhandle's communities, such as De Funiak Springs and Marianna, are much smaller and less busy. To some people, these small towns are the best way to experience Florida. These communities are far from the crowds and busy street festivals found elsewhere in the state.

Northeast Florida

Northeast Florida is bordered by Georgia on the north and the Atlantic Ocean on the east. Northeast Florida starts east of Jefferson County, in the eastern panhandle. To the south, northeast Florida ends just below the city of Ocala.

THE LAND AND WATER

Northeast Florida has many state and national parks. A small part of Georgia's Okefenokee Swamp crosses the state line into Florida. Ocala National Forest lies within the region's boundaries. The St. John's River flows from south to north, directly into Jacksonville.

Water, as seen in the Okefenokee Swamp (left) and Alexander Springs in Ocala National Forest (below), is common in northeast Florida.

Northeast Florida Topography

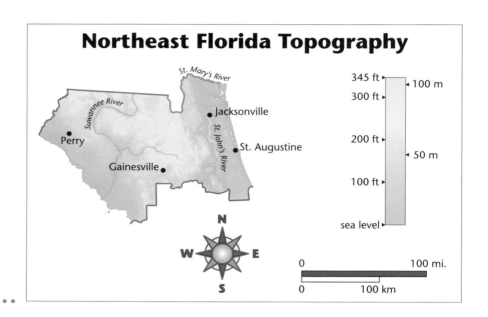

*Western parts of this region are thick with forests. Other land rises and falls gently in green, rounded hilltops. There are some beaches, too, as well as marshy, coastal **lowlands.***

RESOURCES AND AGRICULTURE

Timber is a major resource in northeast Florida. The **commercial** woodlands lie in the western areas. In Alachua County, at the center of this region, close to half of all land is used for crops or pastures. Major crops include beans, tobacco, peanuts, corn, and watermelons.

Way Down upon the Suwannee...

The Suwannee River begins in the Okefenokee Swamp and runs through Florida for 280 miles before emptying into the Gulf of Mexico. This river has 62 **springs.**

Florida's only rapids is on the Suwannee, in Big Shoals State Forest. In the 1780s, parts of the Suwannee Sound were used as hiding places by pirates.

*Marion County, home to the city of Ocala, is famous for its **thoroughbred** horses and horse farms. Farmers in this region also raise beef cattle.*

INDUSTRY

Northeast Florida has a very **diverse** economy. Manufacturers make chemicals, printed materials, and processed foods. Many people work in the insurance, real estate, or financial businesses, including banks. Jacksonville alone **employs** more than 58,000 workers in these types of jobs.

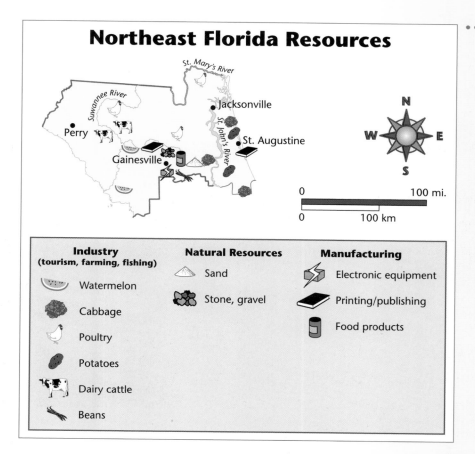

Northeast Florida Resources

Industry
(tourism, farming, fishing)

- Watermelon
- Cabbage
- Poultry
- Potatoes
- Dairy cattle
- Beans

Natural Resources

- Sand
- Stone, gravel

Manufacturing

- Electronic equipment
- Printing/publishing
- Food products

*In addition to the resources seen on the map at left, there is **abundant** timber in this region. Plywood, paper, furniture, and other wood products all come out of northeast Florida in large quantities.*

*There are several factories in this region that process wood into paper. Statewide, the wood and paper industry **employs** 41,000 people.*

Thousands of people in this region work in the service **industry.** This is partly due to the beaches, resorts, and historic cities (such as St. Augustine) that attract tourists.

CITIES AND TOWNS

The many trains and buses in this region make it easy to get from place to place. A train line also runs through Jacksonville and other cities here, but most people still require cars to get where they're going. There are also airports in Jacksonville and Gainesville.

In this part of the state, many people are either going to or coming from Jacksonville. It is an enormous city. With 841 square miles, Jacksonville has the largest land area of any city in the United States. Jacksonville was originally called Cowford. It was just a spot for cows to ford, or cross, the St. John's River. The city grew up

Jacksonville is a major port for boats and ships. It is also the home of a United States naval air station.

The Spanish-built Castillo de San Marcos was constructed between 1672 and 1695 in St. Augustine.

around its seaport, which now is among the busiest ports in the nation. The Jacksonville Naval Air Station is one of two navy bases nearby.

Gainesville, a little farther south, is the home of the University of Florida. This university has 40,000 students. It is known for its many learning programs, including classes in medicine and agriculture, and its sports teams. In the past, Gainesville was much smaller. It was once called Hogtown because there were many hogs nearby.

St. Augustine, on Florida's east coast, is the oldest city in the United States that was settled by Europeans. Among its most famous sights is the Castillo de San Marcos. This fort was built by Spanish **conquistadores.** They used a local stone called coquina, which is made mostly from seashells, to construct the fort. Visitors can cross the fort's moat and walk along its walls.

Micanopy

The small town of Micanopy is only about ten miles south of Gainesville, but it is a very different place. It is named after Micanopy, a leader of the Seminole Nation. Micanopy is not nearly as busy as Gainesville. Most cars are driven by tourists who come to buy **antiques** in the shops that line the main street. At night, hours sometimes go by without a single car passing.

The town has buildings and homes that are at least 100 years old, including the beautiful Herlong Mansion. For overnight visitors in Micanopy, the most popular thing to do is just relax. Micanopy often seems like a place stuck in time, without modern-day hustle and bustle.

Central Florida

Central Florida, with its many attractions, is a destination for millions of tourists. In some ways, however, it is an area largely unexplored, even by state residents.

This region stretches like a belt across the center of Florida, about 100 miles from coast to coast. On the west are the Gulf of Mexico and two of the state's major cities, Tampa and St. Petersburg. On the east are the Atlantic Ocean and the Kennedy Space Center. Orlando is in the middle. Most of Florida's famous orange groves are also in this area.

THE LAND AND WATER

Two of the bodies of water that give Florida's map a **distinct** appearance are in central Florida. Tampa Bay, on the west coast, is shaped like a small boomerang. Lake Okeechobee lies to the southeast,

Lake Okeechobee

Lake Okeechobee is **vital** to Floridians in many ways. Most importantly, it is a backup water supply for millions of residents. When the lake falls below normal levels, government officials often impose water **restrictions** on homes and businesses.

The lake is also an important source of tourism and recreation. Fishermen call it "the Big O." They bring boats there from all over the state to fish for bass.

and is the second-largest **freshwater** lake entirely within the **continental United States** (Lake Michigan is the largest). Lake Okeechobee gives Florida's map a large "hole" in the middle.

Other bodies of freshwater in central Florida include rivers, **springs,** and marshes. There are also close to 3,000 lakes.

RESOURCES AND AGRICULTURE

One of every three acres in Florida, more than 10 million of the state's 35 million acres, is farmed. Many of those farms are in central Florida. Six Florida counties use more than 70 percent of their land for farms, and all of these counties are in central Florida. More than 84 percent of Hardee County is farmland, the highest percentage in the state.

Central Florida Topography

Central Florida is home to two of Florida's largest lakes. Lake George is in the northernmost part of the region, and Lake Okeechobee is in the southernmost part.

Most of Florida's citrus crops, including oranges, grapefruit, and tangerines, are grown here. Florida is the nation's largest citrus grower. After Brazil, it is the second-largest citrus grower in the world.

The climate is a few degrees warmer here than in the northeast, especially in winter. Around the inland citrus groves, and in Orlando, the weather is often more humid. There is a lot of rain during the summer season, when some areas receive as much as 24 inches of rain.

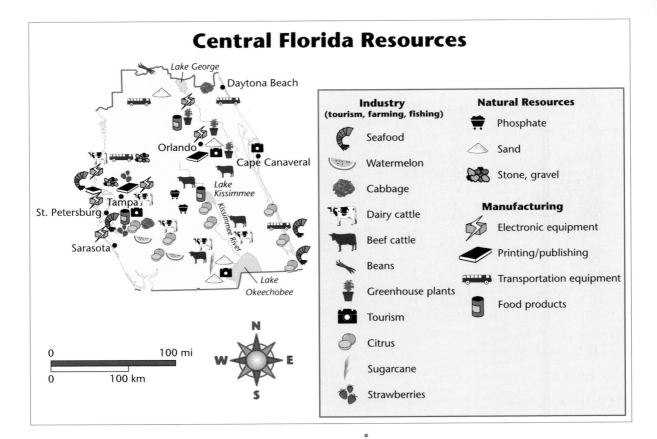

Central Florida Resources

Lake George
Daytona Beach
Orlando
Cape Canaveral
Lake Kissimmee
Kissimmee River
Tampa
St. Petersburg
Sarasota
Lake Okeechobee

Industry
(tourism, farming, fishing)

- Seafood
- Watermelon
- Cabbage
- Dairy cattle
- Beef cattle
- Beans
- Greenhouse plants
- Tourism
- Citrus
- Sugarcane
- Strawberries

Natural Resources

- Phosphate
- Sand
- Stone, gravel

Manufacturing

- Electronic equipment
- Printing/publishing
- Transportation equipment
- Food products

0   100 mi
0   100 km

N W E S

Commercial fishing is important here. Florida's second largest seafood-producing county, Pinellas County (which includes the city of St. Petersburg), produces more than twelve million pounds of fish, shrimp, and oysters each year.

INDUSTRY

The service **industry** is one of the largest in central Florida. Orange County is home to Florida's two largest theme parks. Walt Disney World Resort **employs** about 55,000 workers. Universal Studios employs more than 14,000 people. They serve food, help people off rides, and plan **finances.** Thousands of residents work in these and other service jobs.

About 75 percent of this country's **phosphate** comes from central Florida. Cattle ranching is common here, and manufacturing and shipping contribute money to this region as well.

This phosphate fertilizer plant in east Tampa provides many jobs for area residents.

Walt Disney World Resort, in Orlando, is one of the world's most visited attractions.

CITIES AND TOWNS

The best known city here is Orlando, which was a farming community until Walt Disney built his theme park. Each year, Disney World attracts more than 35 million visitors. Orlando is also home to Universal Studios and SeaWorld.

Daytona Beach, home of Bethune-Cookman College, lies in the northeast corner of this region. **NASCAR** fans flock to the International Speedway for car races.

Farther south, Titusville and Cocoa Beach support the workers at nearby Kennedy Space Center. This part of Florida is called "the Space Coast."

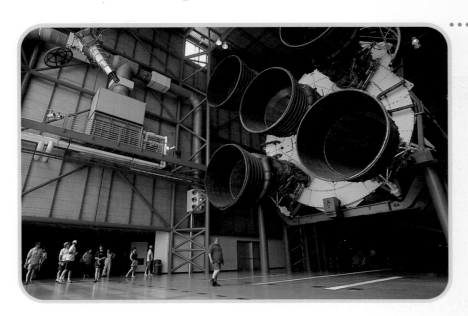

This Saturn V rocket engine—a part of the rocket that took astronauts to the moon—is on display at the Kennedy Space Center.

27

The Ringling Museum of the Circus was established in 1948. It was the first of its kind to display the history of the circus in the United States.

Tampa and St. Petersburg, on the west coast of this region, are so close to each other that local residents often call them by one name—Tampa-St. Pete. Busch Gardens, home of the nation's fourth-largest zoo, can be found there, as can the Sunken Gardens, which showcase **tropical** plants and wildlife.

There are also top professional sports teams in this area of Florida, such as the Orlando Magic, as well as many museums. One **unique** museum displays works by the famous Spanish **surrealist** painter, Salvador Dalí.

Sarasota, farther south, was settled by Scottish **immigrants** in the late 1800s. Today, it is known for its many fine beaches and the Ringling Museum of the Circus.

In today's central Florida, the city and the country exist comfortably, side by side.

Southwest Florida

Southwest Florida is not as populated as Florida's other regions, but thousands of retired senior citizens live here along a strip of coastline on the Gulf of Mexico. Recently, more people have also been moving to this region. In addition to several medium-sized cities, this area also has the state's most **remote** communities, located in the Everglades. Much of that region is almost completely unoccupied by humans. Instead, it is home to alligators, bald eagles, tree snails, orchids, and deer.

Alligators are a common sight around the wet areas of southwest Florida.

Big Cypress National Preserve is protected by the federal government to keep it safe for future generations to enjoy.

THE LAND AND WATER

Southwest Florida's natural environment is one of its most interesting features. The land is very flat and wet, extending to the far southern tip of the state. More than half of this region is protected by the federal government. Everglades National Park makes up a large part of this natural area, and the Big Cypress National **Preserve** sits above the northern border of the Everglades. There are also thousands of small islands here.

Everglades Park is totally **unique.** It looks like a huge swamp that goes on as far as you can see. Actually, however, the Everglades is a very shallow, slow-moving river that flows south, starting from Lake Okeechobee. It washes over a rough-edged grass, called sawgrass, that grows nearly everywhere in the Everglades. This is why the Everglades has been called a "river of grass."

Many trees, like these Dwarf Cypress trees, grow in the swampy lands of the Everglades.

Big Cypress National Preserve is also home to sawgrass and alligators. Most of the water in the preserve, however, stands still.

RESOURCES AND AGRICULTURE

There is one **abundant** resource here that is unusual. This is the mangrove. Mangroves are thin, treelike plants that grow near muddy coastal areas where the water is salty. Fish such as the mangrove snapper, as well as crocodiles, frogs, pelicans, and other wildlife, depend on the mangroves in order to live. They use the mangroves for protection from predators, and find food among their roots.

Southwest Florida also has a fair amount of agriculture. Many muddy inland areas have been turned into farms that grow sugarcane, peppers, cucumbers, and tomatoes. The citrus business is important here, too.

The climate in southwest Florida is wet. About 26 inches of rain fall during July and August. August highs are usually around 91°F, and the low temperature in January is a little more than 53°F.

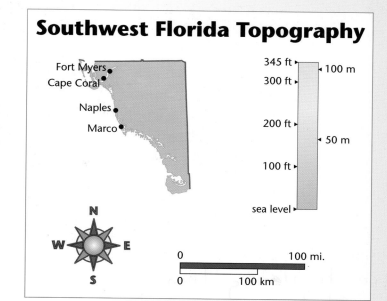

Southwest Florida Topography

Fort Myers
Cape Coral
Naples
Marco

345 ft — 100 m
300 ft
200 ft — 50 m
100 ft
sea level

N
W   E
S

0   100 mi.
0   100 km

Southwest Florida's land is not far above sea level. Much of this region is covered with water.

The Ten Thousand Islands, along the coast of southwest Florida, attract many fishers every year.

Southwest Florida Resources

Fort Myers

Naples

Industry
(tourism, farming, fishing)

Seafood

Watermelon

Beef cattle

Citrus

Sugarcane

Manufacturing

Printing/publishing

N W E S

0   100 mi.

0   100 km

Southwest Florida also attracts thousands of tourists each year because of its many resorts, beaches, and excellent fishing opportunities.

INDUSTRY

Most people work in the service sector. Boats, boat supplies, and seafood processing provide other jobs. People in Collier and Lee Counties produce seafood. Lee County is the third-largest seafood producer in Florida.

Southwest Florida's economy is strong and most people live well. This is partly because many retired people have saved enough money to live there very comfortably.

CITIES AND TOWNS

Fort Myers, in Lee County, is the region's largest city. Thomas Edison had his winter home there. His

Lightning Capital

Florida is the lightning capital of the United States. The state is struck by lightning more than any other state in the nation. It makes sense, then, that more people die in Florida from being struck by lightning than in any other state.

    Because southwest Florida is so rainy, this region is among the areas of the state that receive the most lightning strikes. Electricity that builds up in rain clouds sometimes hits the earth as lightning. Southeast Florida and central Florida also have frequent, fierce lightning storms during the summer months.

inventions include the electric lightbulb and the phonograph, a type of early record player.

Naples, in Collier County, is known for its powder-white beaches. Also nearby are the Caribbean Gardens, Collier Seminole State Park, and the Collier County Museum.

This photograph shows the laboratory of inventor Thomas Edison's winter home in Fort Myers.

If you want to visit one of Florida's most **remote** communities, Flamingo, you'll have to take a long drive. People who like to fish are usually the only ones who travel there. Flamingo sits at the end of a long road at the very bottom of Everglades National Park. Like the southwest region itself, Flamingo can be a great place to go if you enjoy nature.

Sanibel and Captiva Islands

Two of Florida's most popular islands are off the coast near Fort Myers. These are Sanibel and Captiva Islands. They are popular with tourists who want to relax on the beach and eat fresh seafood.

These islands are two of the best places in North America to collect seashells. Every time the tide comes in, thousands of seashells ride in with it. Seashell hunting is very common. Locals joke that tourists develop a medical condition known as the "Sanibel Stoop" from bending over to pick up shells.

Southeast Florida

Busy southeast Florida has attracted many of its residents from around the country and around the world. People come to this area for the good jobs (the economy is very strong), the warm weather and sunshine, and the many things to do. People from Latin America and the Caribbean are common here, and their **cultures** and traditions have contributed much to the area. There is something to do in southeast Florida any time of the day or night.

Miami, southeast Florida's largest city, sponsors a festival each year called the Calle Ocho Festival. Here, you can try food and listen to music from all over Latin America.

Some people worry that too many houses and businesses have been built in southeast Florida. Developments such as this one could harm natural **habitats.**

THE LAND AND WATER

Southeast Florida once looked a lot like southwest Florida—it was very wet. Much of the region still is. The difference is that more people have chosen to live in southeast Florida. **Development** companies have drained large sections of swampy land and filled them in with earth. They have even created entirely new islands in Biscayne Bay. Brand-new communities have been built on top of formerly swampy land.

Along the Atlantic coast, wide beaches are a common sight. The sand on the state's east coast tends to look a little more brown and feel more coarse than the west coast beaches. The Atlantic coastline sometimes has waves for surfers and others who enjoy the surf.

One important natural feature of southeast Florida

Southeast Florida's topography is flat, and does not rise far above sea level. Much damage can be done to the area during **tropical** *storms.*

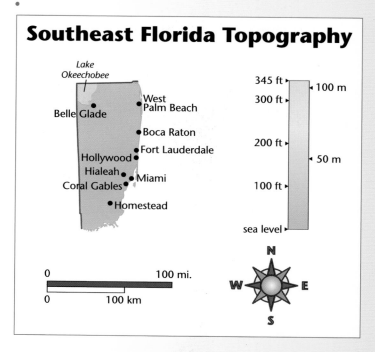

Southeast Florida Topography

Fish swim through a coral cave in Biscayne National Park. The largest mangrove forest remaining on Florida's east coast is also within the park's boundaries.

sits under the water—its **coral reefs.** Some of the most **extensive** coral reefs in the world are here, and they attract thousands of **scuba divers** and **snorkelers.** One national park south of Miami is almost entirely underwater—Biscayne National Park. There, you can ride boats to the coral reefs and rent equipment to view the **spectacular** undersea life.

RESOURCES AND AGRICULTURE

You might expect to find little agriculture in such a heavily populated region as this, but almost half of Palm Beach County's land is used for agriculture. Enormous sugarcane plantations have made Florida the nation's leading sugarcane producer. Southeast Florida's other crops include strawberries, tomatoes, sweet corn, cucumbers, celery, and avocados.

In 2000 and 2001, **citrus canker** infected many trees in the region's citrus groves. Thousands of trees were cut down to try to stop the canker from spreading to other groves. Today, only a few groves remain here.

This region's climate is similar to southwest Florida, though it is a bit cooler in the summer and a little warmer in the winter. Summer rainfall totals average just under twenty inches during July and August.

In addition to growing food crops like sugarcane and strawberries, farmers in southeast Florida also grow greenhouse plants. The city of Miami is also one of the country's largest clothing producers.

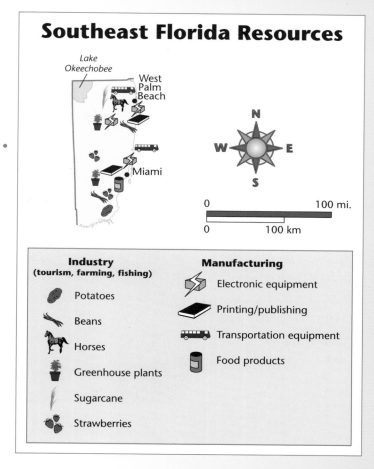

Southeast Florida Resources

Lake Okeechobee

West Palm Beach

Miami

N W E S

| 0 | 100 mi. |

| 0 | 100 km |

Industry
(tourism, farming, fishing)

- Potatoes
- Beans
- Horses
- Greenhouse plants
- Sugarcane
- Strawberries

Manufacturing

- Electronic equipment
- Printing/publishing
- Transportation equipment
- Food products

INDUSTRY

The service **industry** provides most of the jobs in southeast Florida. Hundreds of thousands of workers are required to keep everything running for the millions of residents and millions of tourists. In the Miami area alone, more than 362,000 people work in the service industry. Employers here include the University of Miami, with nearly 8,000 workers; American Express in Fort Lauderdale, a credit card company, with 5,000 people; and the seafood industry in Palm Beach, Broward, and Miami-Dade Counties, which together produce millions of pounds of seafood each year.

Wet and Dry Seasons

People say that south Florida has two seasons—wet and dry.

The dry season runs from about mid-October through mid-May. This is also when the **humidity** is lowest and the temperatures are most pleasant.

The wet, or rainy, season runs from late spring until early fall. This is a time of year when smart residents keep umbrellas handy.

*Owners of sugarcane plantations and other agricultural businesses **employ** thousands of workers in southeast Florida.*

Banking, trade, and financial services are also important **industries** in southeast Florida. This is partly because the region is so near countries in Latin America and the Caribbean. Companies in those nations often do a lot of business in Miami.

With all this industry, southeast Florida's economy is strong. This is usually true even when the national economy is struggling. The presence of many wealthy people in southeast Florida has given the region a nickname: the "Gold Coast." However, despite the strong economy, some people in southeast Florida don't earn very much money. This is because many service jobs don't pay high salaries. They often pay only minimum wage, which is the lowest amount of money employers are allowed to pay by law.

CITIES AND TOWNS

In this region's communities, you can dance with people from all over Latin America at street festivals and sip the milk directly from a coconut. You can mingle with big-time movie stars and singers. Or, you can just lie on the beach. The cities and towns here offer many choices.

In West Palm Beach, tourists mix with locals along busy Clematis Street, which is lined with shops and restaurants. Palm Beach is just across a strip of water called the Intracoastal Waterway. Wealthy people began to live in Palm Beach starting in the late 1800s. Today, some of the nation's wealthiest families own mansions near the Atlantic Ocean and shop in the expensive stores on Worth Avenue.

Huge homes, like the one below in Palm Beach, are evidence of southeast Florida's well-to-do residents. Palm Beach's Worth Avenue, at right, has many expensive stores.

Little Havana

The city of Miami has a neighborhood known as Little Havana. Beginning in the 1950s and 1960s, Cuban **immigrants** had a lot of influence in this area. The streets that you walk there look like they are in Cuba.

The heart of Little Havana is Eighth Street, or *Calle Ocho* as it is known in Spanish. It's an interesting place, filled with bustling Cuban restaurants, small stores, and music.

Broward and Miami-Dade Counties, to the south, have very **diverse immigrant** populations. Many residents come from Latin American and Caribbean countries, including Haiti, Jamaica, Cuba, and Brazil. This area is full of restaurants and stores that sell food and products found in those countries. Many people like to visit this region just to experience these qualities.

Fort Lauderdale's Las Olas Boulevard has many shops, restaurants, and cafes. One end of the street is downtown, and the other stops beside the Atlantic Ocean.

Fort Lauderdale, in Broward County, has become one of the region's most active spots. The city was named for Major William Lauderdale, who built a fort in the area in 1838 during the **Second Seminole War.** People come from all over the world to visit, particularly from Europe and Canada. Fort Lauderdale is famous for its beaches and its **nightlife.** Residents and visitors attend concerts, dinners, art exhibits, and festivals in Fort Lauderdale.

Miami, with a population of almost 400,000, attracts millions of visitors each year. Its buildings and colorful lights paint the skyline.

Passengers constantly come and go from huge cruise ships. Miami is one of the world's largest cruise ports. Just across Biscayne Bay from Miami, Miami Beach draws some of the world's most famous people. Many stars have been photographed around this community's best-known area: South Beach.

The skyline of downtown Miami at night is bright and beautiful. There is always something fun to do in this part of Florida.

Southeast Florida's other communities include Homestead, which is home to Coral Castle, a house built entirely of coral, and the Homestead Air Force Base; Hollywood, a resort and residential community near the Hollywood Seminole Indian Reservation; and Coral Gables, home of the University of Miami.

The Biltmore Hotel, in Coral Gables, Florida, has been attracting visitors since 1926. It is now a national historic landmark.

The Keys

The Florida Keys—the hundreds of islands just to the south and west of the southern tip of Florida's **mainland**—are entirely **unique** (map page 45). There is no place else like them on Earth. The term "key" comes from the Spanish word *cayo,* which means "rocky island." The Keys are linked to the mainland by the Overseas Highway, which has 42 bridges and more than 100 miles of road. The Keys dangle in the ocean like a chain of land.

THE LAND AND WATER

Each key has its own **distinct** shape, but all are narrow strips of land made from pieces of coral. They rise only a few feet above sea level. The islands look as flat as pancakes, and are covered with sand and **tropical** vegetation.

The Overseas Highway stretches out over the ocean in Florida's Keys. The highway runs where a railroad used to be.

The most common water is seawater. You can often see the Gulf of Mexico on one side of an island and the Atlantic Ocean on the other at the same

time. Drinking water comes from Florida's mainland in a pipe. **Coral reefs** surround the Keys in the water.

RESOURCES AND AGRICULTURE

The Keys have no farms. The soil here is very sandy, but there are few beaches. Mostly, the land just stops and the sea begins.

The climate, average temperatures, and rainfall totals are nearly identical to those in southeast Florida. However, since the Keys are small and surrounded by the ocean, they often enjoy cool breezes.

Florida Keys Resources

Key Largo

Marathon

Key West

0   50 mi.

0   50 km

Industry
(tourism, farming, fishing)

Tourism

Seafood

Manufacturing
Printing/publishing

Florida's Keys make most of their money from the fishing and tourist industries.

Hurricanes

The Keys are especially **vulnerable** to dangerous hurricanes. Hurricanes are powerful **tropical** storms with continuous winds of at least 74 miles per hour. Strong hurricanes can rip apart buildings and kill anyone who isn't protected.

The Florida peninsula also has suffered many of these storms, but hurricanes can seem most frightening on the **remote** islands of the Keys. Here, residents are entirely surrounded by an angry sea.

*Scuba divers and **snorkelers** come from around the world to enjoy Florida's Keys.*

INDUSTRY

The Keys depend on tourists to keep their economy strong. People work as **scuba** instructors, fishing guides, and waiters. **Commercial** fishing is important here. Monroe County leads Florida in annual seafood production.

CITIES AND TOWNS

The best known town is Key West, at the far end of the Overseas Highway. Key West has long been popular with writers and artists, including the famous American novelist Ernest Hemingway and playwright Tennessee Williams.

The Seven-Mile Bridge leads to Marathon. Islamorada is on the way as you drive from Key West back toward Miami. Both Marathon and Islamorada are well-known among sport fishers, boaters, and scuba divers. Key Largo is the closest key to the **mainland.** Scuba divers love nearby John Pennekamp **Coral Reef** State Park, which is home to a great variety of underwater life.

*Cuba lies just 90 miles to the south of this marker, which shows the southernmost point of the **continental United States.***

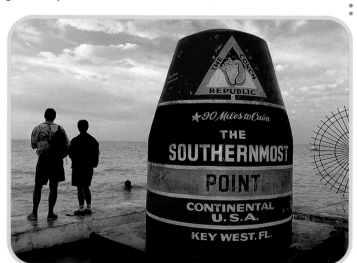

Map of Florida

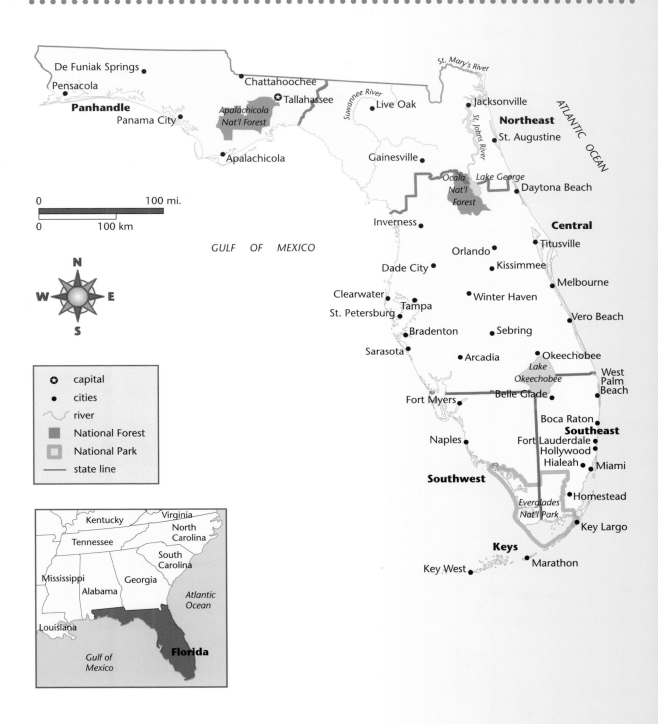

De Funiak Springs
Pensacola
Panhandle
Panama City
Chattahoochee
Tallahassee
Apalachicola Nat'l Forest
Apalachicola
Suwannee River
Live Oak
St. Mary's River
Jacksonville
Northeast
St. Augustine
ATLANTIC OCEAN
Gainesville
St. Johns River
Lake George
Ocala Nat'l Forest
Daytona Beach
Inverness
Central
Titusville
Orlando
Kissimmee
Melbourne
Dade City
GULF OF MEXICO
Clearwater
Winter Haven
Tampa
St. Petersburg
Vero Beach
Bradenton
Sebring
Sarasota
Arcadia
Okeechobee
Lake Okeechobee
West Palm Beach
Fort Myers
Belle Glade
Boca Raton
Naples
Southeast
Fort Lauderdale
Hollywood
Hialeah
Miami
Southwest
Homestead
Everglades Nat'l Park
Key Largo
Keys
Key West
Marathon

0   100 mi.
0   100 km

N
W   E
S

⊙ capital
• cities
    river
    National Forest
    National Park
    state line

Kentucky
Virginia
Tennessee
North Carolina
Mississippi
Alabama
Georgia
South Carolina
Louisiana
Atlantic Ocean
Gulf of Mexico
Florida

45

Glossary

abundant plentiful

antique collectible object valued partly because it is old

Appalachian Mountains mountain chain in North America that runs 2,000 miles from Canada to central Alabama

charter boat boat that can be rented to take people fishing

citrus canker disease that leaves brown spots on oranges, grapefruits, and other citrus fruits

commercial having to do with business; not for personal use

conquistador Spanish explorer who came to Florida looking for gold

continental United States all states except Alaska and Hawaii, which are separated from the other states by ocean or land

coral reef large, underwater object made up of the colorful shells of thousands of tiny living sea creatures

culture art, music, beliefs, and ideas of a group of people

dense packed tightly together

development construction of homes, businesses, roads, and other things that serve a community

distinct unusual and different

diverse varied

employ to hire or have working for

extensive far-reaching

finance having to do with money

freshwater water that has little or no salt in it and can be used for drinking; this type of water is found in most lakes and rivers

habitat place perfectly suited to a particular animal or plant

humidity amount of water in the air

hydroelectric dam dam that changes the power of moving water into electricity

immigrant person who moves from one country to live in another

industry manufacturing and other businesses located in an area

International Space Station large station being built in space with the cooperation of sixteen different countries. When complete, the station will weigh one million pounds and be home to an international crew of seven people who will live and work in space for up to six months at a time.

lowland area of land that is flat and low

mainland main part of a continent, as opposed to an offshore island or group of islands

mineral rock-like material that comes from the ground with its own special color, hardness, and structure

NASCAR (National Association for Stock Car Automobile Racing) organization formed in 1948 to organize car races

natural resource anything found in nature that humans consider necessary, like air, plants, animals, minerals, and water. Natural resources can be renewable (they make more of themselves, like plants, if given the chance) or non-renewable (they cannot make more of themselves, like coal).

nightlife restaurants, stores, and theaters that are usually open after other places close for the night

phosphate material that is mined from a rock and made into fertilizers

preserve protected area for plants and animals that is set aside by people

pulp wood from a tree that is treated with chemicals to make paper

quartz type of see-through mineral

remote far away from other places

restriction law or rule saying you cannot do or use something without limits

scuba diver person who swims under water while breathing air from a tank

Second Seminole War (1835–1842) second in a series of three wars fought by the United States Army against Florida's Seminole Indians. The army was trying to take land away from the Seminole so that United States settlers could move there.

snorkeler person who uses a snorkel, or long thin tube, to breathe while swimming on top of the water

spectacular astonishing

spring source of water that comes up through the ground

subtropical warm, wet area on Earth next to the tropical zone

surrealist artist whose works emphasize dreams and creativity. This art was popular from the 1920s to the 1940s. These artists emphasized the unexpected by putting things that didn't belong together in the same piece of art.

thoroughbred horse that has been specially bred to run races

timber trees used for making paper, furniture, and other wood products

tropical hot, wet area near Earth's equator that never experiences frost and where plants grow year-round

unique unlike anything else

vital absolutely necessary

vulnerable able to be hurt in some way

wired hooked up to the Internet and the worldwide web

More Books to Read

Chui, Patricia. *Florida: The Sunshine State.* Milwaukee, Wisc.: Gareth Stevens Inc., 2002.

Heinrichs, Ann. *Florida.* Danbury, Conn.: Children's Press, 1998.
     An older reader can help you with this book.

Russell, William. *The Florida Keys.* Vero Beach, FL: The Rourke Book Company, 1994.

Thompson, Kathleen. *Florida.* N.Y.: Raintree Steck-Vaughn, 1996.

Index

About the Author

Bob Knotts is an author and playwright who lives near Fort Lauderdale. He has published 24 novels and nonfiction books for both young readers and adults. He also writes for several top national magazines.